Kate and Tom Learn About Fossil Fuels

DINOSAURS AND FOSSIL CARBON

CHILDREN SAVING OUR PLANET SERIES

CAROL SUTTERS

Illustrated by William Fong

AuthorHouse™ UK
1663 Liberty Drive
Bloomington, IN 47403 USA
www.authorhouse.co.uk
UK TFN: 0800 0148641 (Toll Free inside the UK)
UK Local: 02036 956322 (+44 20 3695 6322 from outside the UK)

This book is printed on acid-free paper.

ISBN: 978-1-6655-8603-0 (sc)
ISBN: 978-1-6655-8602-3 (e)

Library of Congress Control Number: 2021903230

Print information available on the last page.

Published by AuthorHouse 03/30/2021

authorHOUSE®

The day after the demonstration at the Houses of Parliament to save the planet, Mum suggested that Kate and Tom need to learn about green carbon and fossil carbon.

Mum says, "We *will not travel by aeroplane to Scotland this year as we want to reduce our carbon footprint and cause less pollution. Air travel uses fossil fuel for energy.*"

"Alterative travel could be less harmful to animals and birds and cause less damage to the world we live in."

"What is all that about carbon", says Tom?

Mum says, *"A carbon footprint is the amount of carbon pollution we cause when we do something that uses fossil carbon. This results in excess carbon gas called carbon dioxide in the air. This causes the climate to change and has damaging effects on the earth."*

Oil Wells

"We need to choose ways to do things that use less of the fossil fuels from the earth. Fossil fuels are coal, gas and oil. Coal comes from coal mines. Gas from within the earth and oil from oil well on the earth or in the sea."

"We need to find a new way to lower our carbon footprints, as I will explain later. Damage to the environment only happens when we use fossil carbon not green carbon."

Triceratops

Tyrannosaurus
Rex

"Fossil carbon comes from fossil fuel which was formed over a 100 million years when dinosaurs and plants were buried in the earth. Over time their bodies broke down in the earth so the carbon in their bodies together with that of other animals and plants got trapped and were later turned into fossil fuels."

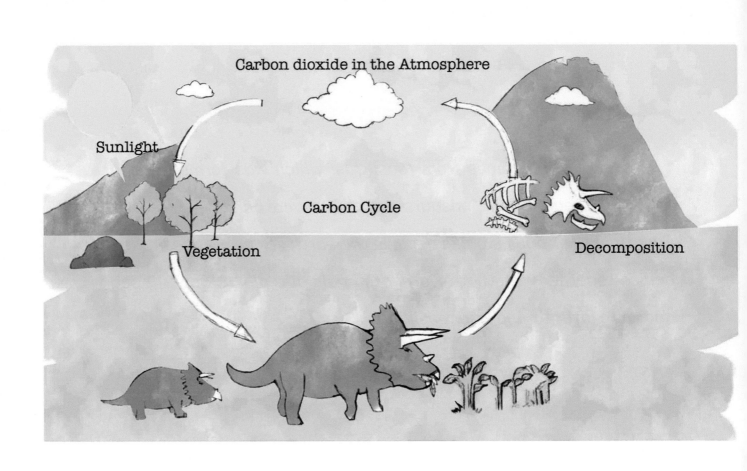

"Is all carbon dioxide bad?", says Kate.

"No", says mum.

"We have a normal carbon cycle on our earth which is important for us to live. This is called Green Carbon that is the good carbon."

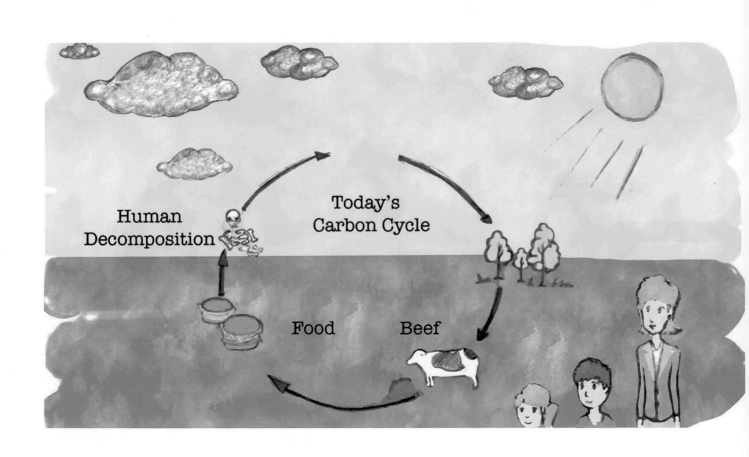

"*The earth's air contains carbon dioxide which is very important for keeping us warm. The carbon cycle balances the carbon in the air, the oceans and the earth. It is vital for us to live.*"

"There was seven times the amount of carbon dioxide in the Jurassic age when dinosaurs lived."

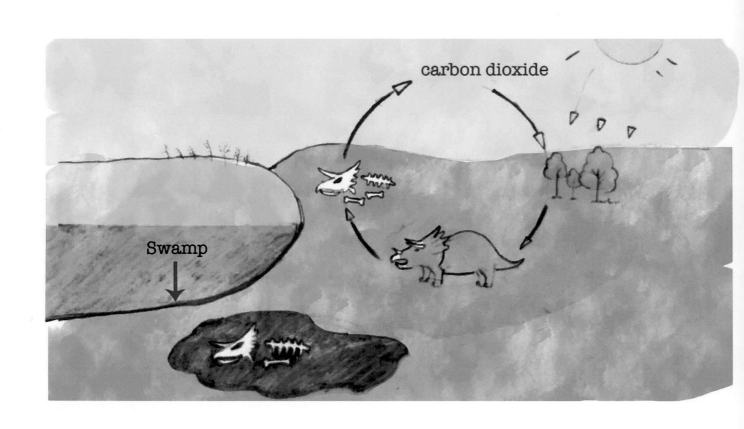

"It was very hot when the dinosaurs were alive in the Jurassic period. The decomposition of animals and plants and sea creatures releases the carbon back into the atmosphere."

"After many years the decomposition of dinosaurs stopped working in swamps and where green algae grows. When the decomposition did not work the carbon in these plants and animals sank into the ground and the heat and pressure made it into oil and coal."

"In the meantime, over millions of years the carbon cycle on earth changed, so that there is now a lot less carbon in the air than when the dinosaurs lived on earth."

"So today when we burn oil or coal there is a big concentration of carbon, which is in excess of what we need in the air and this causes pollution and affects climate. These fossil fuels contain energy from sunlight trapped millions of years ago.

Fossil carbon as a source of energy is the thing that causes climate change and extreme weather."

What did we learn today? (tick the box if you understood and agree)

☐ There is a normal way in which carbon gets recycled and this is called the CARBON CYCLE.

☐ Dinosaurs decaying in the swamps and getting buried with plants over millions of years made fossil carbons like coal and oil.

☐ Burning fossil fuels causes excess carbon dioxide in the air and this is air pollution.

☐ We should try to reduce our carbon footprint in our everyday lives.

Read how Tom and Kate choose Green carbon in Book 3.

Children Saving our Planet Series

Books

1. **Tom and Kate Go to Westminster**

2. **Kate and Tom Learn About Fossil Fuels**

3. **Tom and Kate Chose Green Carbon**

4. **Tress and Deforestation**

5. **Our Neighbourhood Houses**

6. **Our Neighbourhood Roads**

7. **Shopping at the Farm Shop**

8. **Travelling to a Holiday by the Sea**

9. **Picnic at the Seaside on Holiday**

10. **The Oceans and Coral**

11. **Our Carbon Footprint**

12. **Fire Fire**

13. **The Antartic Warms Up**

14. **The Canada Catastrophe**

15. **The Coronavirus and saving the Planet**

16. **The Children's Rebellion and Climate Change**

These series of simple books explain the landmark importance of Children's participation in the Extinction rebellion protest. Children actively want to encourage and support adults to urgently tackle both the Climate and the Biodiversity emergencies. The booklets enable children at an early age to understand some of the scientific principles that are affecting the destruction of the planet. If global political and economic systems fail to address the climate emergency, the responsibility will rest upon children to save the Planet for themselves.

This series is dedicated to Theodore, Aria and Ophelia.

Printed in the United States
by Baker & Taylor Publisher Services